Happy Frugal Student

by

Rachel Henderson

Copyright © Rachel Henderson 2013

Happy Frugal Student by Rachel Henderson

Contents

Contents...2

Introduction 5

Financial Education 6

    Why financial skills are important 6

    Financial Advice 8

        Financial Institutions 8

        Financial Advisors 9

        Family and Friends 9

    The Cost of Debt 10

    How to keep a budget...11

    How to repay debt 14

Student Loan..15

    Good and Bad Debt...16

    Vocational Courses 17

    Other Courses 17

    To Borrow or not to Borrow?...20

Topping up the Loan 21

    Borrowing Extra 22

Happy Frugal Student by Rachel Henderson

- Using savings 24
- Help From Parents 24
- Earning Money 25
- How to spend less money 27
  - Course Fees 27
  - Rent 28
  - Bills 29
  - Food 31
  - Travel 32
  - Books & Stationery 34
  - Phone 35
  - Insurance 37
  - Other Items 38
- Student Discounts 38
- Other Discounts 39
- Savings Account 41
- Happiness 42
- Appendix 1 45
  - Simple Pasta 45
  - Bolognaise 45

Happy Frugal Student by Rachel Henderson

    Jacket Potatoes 46

    Vegetable and Bean stew 46

    Easy Curry 47

    Macaroni Cheese 47

    Sausage and Beans 48

Appendix 2 49

Introduction

Being a student is an important time for many young people. It is the first time that they get to move away from and be independent. They will learn a lot of new things, such as coping socially, cooking and managing finances. Some will take away valuable lessons but others will get in to bad habits that will remain with them. This is why it is so important to take a look at this book on finance and hopefully get in to good spending habits right from the beginning. By forming good habits you will not only leave university with less debt but you will also have started great habits to continue for the rest of your life.

The book starts off by explaining about what a financial education is and what basics everyone should know. It then discusses student loans and other ways of financing student life. It follows with tips on how to reduce spending. Lastly it has information on savings accounts and how to be frugal and happy.

Financial Education

Unfortunately, in school, many of us do not get much of a financial education. We are not taught about saving, debts, loan repayments and managing a budget and this is left to parents to teach us. Some parents do not teach this and others do not manage their finances that well and so do not have much to teach. Some unfortunately teach the wrong things or set a bad example. However, it is possible to teach yourself, if you have not got a good grounding.

It is good to have an understanding of the importance of good financial skills and well as knowing what those are. The basics are explained below.

Why financial skills are important

If you do not develop good financial skills then you could end up being in debt a lot. This may not be a cause for concern for some people, but it is important to understand the consequences of debt. Some people turn a blind eye to debt and others think that it is not a problem.

Debt costs money. If you borrow money, you have to pay a fee, in the way of interest and possibly other costs as well. These costs can add up. If you use a credit card to pay for an item and do not repay it for a month, then you will be charged a month's interest. For simplicity lets say the item was £100 and the interest is 10% APR. This means that you will pay 83p for the loan and so the item cost you roughly £101. That may not seem much, but imagine you didn't pay it back for a year. It would cost you £106. Or perhaps you didn't pay it back for the term of your course – 3 years. That would cost you £116 after the three years. Imagine you borrowed £1000 then that would be £1053 for a year or £1155 back after three years. These are very low figures though it is more likely that thousands of pounds a year will be borrowed and the interest rate could be a lot higher.

It is very easy to get a collection of store cards and credit cards, which may have interest rates of up to 15%. Then by accumulating debt over the time that you are university and adding on the interest you could easily end up with thousands of pounds worth of debt and possibly no idea how you managed to spend so much.

It is important to remember that with some forms of borrowing, such as a credit card, there is only a minimum amount to pay back each month. This may seem like an advantage as there is less pressure to make a large repayment. However, it means that the loan can hang around for a long time, perhaps even years after you stop being a student. This means that the cost can be huge and with the minimum payments often only covering the interest, you may not be paying back any of what you owe. Then if you miss a repayment, you could end up having the expense of fees on top. Some people find that they can easily ignore their credit card and once they have spent their credit limit on one card they will start using a new card and build up debt on a new one. It can be pretty easy to suddenly become unaware of how many cards you have and how much you owe on each one.

By building up a lot of debt you could end up having a lifetime of repayments. You might even die and leave others to inherit those debts. Having debts could affect your chances of getting certain jobs and your ability to get a mortgage. It could affect your stress levels, relationships and health. It may not seem like a big deal at the time but could lead to much more serious consequences.

It is important to think about the future. It is easy to just assume that you will leave university and find a job that will pay off all of your debts. However, not all graduates get good jobs. You may decide to settle down and have a family instead or find a job that is not that well paid. There are many possibilities where things may not turn out how you expected and you regret not having been more careful with your money. It can be a lot easier than you might think as well.

Financial Advice

If you are looking for financial help, it can be tempting to turn to certain places and assume that they will give you the best possible help. It is important to understand more about these sources of information before you take in everything that they say.

Financial Institutions

In the past everyone trusted the banks. They felt that the staff there would give them the best possible advice for them. More recently, there has been mistrust in the banks due to the fact that they have been found to be selling things to customers without disclosure. This means that people were paying or insurance when they had no idea they were even paying it, so would not have claimed had they needed to or perhaps even would not have ever been eligible to make a claim. Many would not have taken out the insurance had they known. However, despite this, there are still a lot of people that still trust financial institutions to get financial advice. It is so important to understand that people who work in these places are merely salesmen being paid to sell their financial products. They are likely to be on commission and so they will not be looking after the customers by selling them things but just doing it to try to make as much commission as they can.

Financial Advisors

Many financial advisors work free of charge, but get paid from commission on the products that they sell. This means that they are more likely to sell items that will make them a significant amount of money, rather than selling something that might be better for their customers. There are some advisors that charge for consultations and people think that these will be better because they will not need to recommend items for commission as they get paid for their consultation skills. However, they still get commission in the same way and so chances are that they will still be recommending items that will make the more commission and they may just be richer than those advisors that do not charge, rather than being fairer to their customers.

Family and Friends

Although your family and friends will be far more likely to be on your side, with regards to finances, they may still not be the best people to go to for advice. Look carefully at their financial background before you copy what they have done. If they have a lot of money, it could be down to luck or inheritance rather than financial savvy. A lot of people also spend money that they do not have using credit cards and other loans. This can mean that although they appear to be rich, they are not. The best people to go to for advice are those that are happy and frugal.

They know how to minimise spending but still have a good time. Talk to lots of people, but find out how they make their money and what they spend it on, before you decide whether their advice is worth listening to.

The Cost of Debt

So we have established that debts can be expensive and they can hang around for a long time. It is worth noting that some are more expensive than others and this should be considered when looking for debt. Payday loans and unauthorised overdrafts are among the most expensive with credit unions tending to be among the cheapest. When you are considering borrowing, look at the costs; not just the interest rates but also the admin costs, plus any fees that might be charged for late payments and use this to base your decision on. Think about the term as well, because the sooner that you pay something back, the cheaper it is likely to be.

There are many places where you can compare the prices of different loans. These can be a good place to start, but it could be worth talking to a financial advisor or reading a finance book in order to find out about all of the options that are available to you and the advantages and disadvantages of them.

It is also worth considering the non-financial costs. These are things like the stress of having a loan and the cost to your credit rating. If you want to borrow money after university to buy a house, then having loans hanging over you may go against you. Having loan repayments to make may also mean that you cannot afford another loan or even struggle just to pay for day to day things.

You may have to borrow money to afford university but you should be able to keep the amount that you borrow down, more affordable and therefore easier to manage if you are careful.

How to keep a budget

It is so important to know how to keep a budget. This will enable you to make sure that your money lasts.

You firstly need to know how much income you will have. This could be from a student loan plus any savings that you have. It could be from a job you have or money from your parents. Add up all of your sources of income. Things like loans get paid in chunks and savings are there all of the time ready to be spent. This means that it can be tempting to spend a lot at the beginning and then have nothing left at the end of the term or year.

So consider the large chunks of money first. Then think about any regular income that you will also get, such as pay from a job. This will allow you to see how much money you have available to you. You will need to then consider your costs. You may have some chunks of money going out, such as rent if it is paid that way, but also monthly expenses like utility bills. You will also have more variable expenses such as food. It is worth making a note of everything you will have to pay out as well as how much you have coming in.

It is important to understand that some weeks will be dearer than others. If you are travelling to and from home in the holidays then you will have that big cost. You may also need to buy books at the beginning of term, gifts at Christmas, tax and MOT if you have a car and other expenses. You will also have more regular expenses such as utility bills, TV licence, council tax, food, phone and entertainment. You need to consider which are necessary and work out if you can afford them.

If you do not have enough money, then you will need to work out how to get more. You may decide to borrow more, ask your parents for it get a job with better pay or longer hours or cut down your spending so that you can manage.

You will need to look at the money you will have coming in and what you will have to spend on fixed expenses such as rent, utility bills, phone, TV licence, insurance etc. What is left will be there to spend on food, travel, books, entertainment etc. You will be able to set a budget based on how much is left. You may want to set this as a termly budget, monthly or weekly. Consider which you will find easier.

To set a weekly budget can be easier because if you run out early you will not have so long to wait until you can start your next batch of money. So if you spend it all and still have half the time left, you will only have to wait 3 days until you can get some more money. If you are on a monthly budget and have two weeks left before you can get more money, you will have problems as you may not have enough food or fuel to last. Consider what will work better for you based on what you have been used to doing, when your money will be coming in and how well you will be able to manage your money. It does take will power if you have a chunk of money and need to restrict spending to a certain amount each week. You will need to keep a written record of what you are spending in order to do really well, at least to start with. This is especially true if you use credit cards and store cards, which you should pay off in full, as these amounts will be less easy to track.

Happy Frugal Student by Rachel Henderson

It can be easier to just draw out the amount of cash you can spend each week or month and then you will see exactly how much money you have left once you go shopping. Try not to be tempted to use some money from the following week or months budgeted amount as you could end up overspending all of the time. If you have some left over though you might like to put it aside in case you get short at some point. However, once you start to get used to it more, it will be easier. You will start to know how much things cost, how often you buy them and how much you can afford.

It is important to make these decisions before you even start university. Once you do start you will be so busy studying and socialising that you may not find the necessary time to do so. Therefore sort out your finances and your budget beforehand and then you will not have that hassle once you start. You will be able to just concentrate on sticking to that budget.

You may find that once you do start university you find the budget that you have set does not work out. You may find that things are more expensive than you thought or you may find you do not spend as much. If you are going over the budget regularly, work out whether it is possible for you to cut down in any areas. Perhaps you are overspending because you are buying things that are just too expensive or you have miscalculated how much things cost. Go back to your original budget and compare it with what you are spending and check. It may be that you are buying unnecessary items that you can stop buying or that bills are just more than you thought they would be. You may have to change your budget based on this.

If you are not spending as much as you thought you would, this is great. Adjust your budget so that you do not have so much money available to you each week or month and save the difference. Then you will have some money to fall back on, should you need it.

A sample budget is shown in Appendix 2.

How to repay debt

It is also important to understand about repaying debts. While you are a student, you may have a student loan and perhaps also use a credit card, overdraft and other forms of lending. Repaying it could seem almost impossible.

It is easy to forget about repaying debts. Perhaps think that you will worry about that when you get a job or just turn a blind eye completely and not even think about it at all. This could be a big mistake and it is really important to consider debt repayments before you take out any debt.

The student loan repayments will happen automatically. It is not worth worrying about this and best not to repay it early. This is explained in more detail later.

The other loans need to be paid back as soon as possible. It is wise to keep all spending to a minimum and repay as much of the loan as possible, as quickly as possible. Start with the most expensive (taking fees and interest in to account) and do not borrow any more money than necessary. Once you have a job, make sure that you start to pay back loans, rather than borrowing more money. Live well within your means and use extra money to make high repayments so that you can get rid of the debts as quickly as possible.

Some people prefer to start with the smallest loan as they like the feeling that they have managed to pay something off. This will work out dearer but if it works for you, then do it that way. Consider all of your debts and whether you need the quicker reward of having paid some off, rather than working away at the most expensive, which may take longer to repay.

It is important to be strong and use will power to make sure that you pay off the debt rather than spend money on other things. Obviously there will be things that you need, but try not to spend too much on things that you do not need, until you have paid it off.

Hopefully you will have got used to not spending that much money while a student. Try to continue living in this way until all of the debts are paid off. Then save up for things rather than borrowing more money to have them. This will save you a lot of money in the long run. It is also very gratifying to know that you have saved up for something and then bought it. You get a lot more pleasure form it that way. You may also change your mind about buying the item once you have saved up and have no need to spend the money on it. This could save you wasting money on items that you do not really need or want.

It is not easy to go without spending money to pay off a debt. It can feel like you are spending money with nothing to show for it. However, try to remind yourself of the things that you bought with the money that you borrowed and remember that you have to pay for them. Thinking about this may even help you to spend less as if you have not used the items that you bought you may regret buying them in the first place.

Student Loan

We are often told that we should avoid getting in to debt as much as possible. However, student loans are positively encouraged and it can seem strange. To understand this, it is important to understand the difference between good and bad debt.

Good and Bad Debt

Good debt will allow you to get something that will benefit you. This could be borrowing to buy a house that will increase in value far more than the cost of loan. It could be buying a car that will allow you to travel to a job that will massively increase your income. It could mean getting a student loan so that you can get a job that will pay you significantly more money than if you did not do the course.

A student loan is not always good debt. However, if it gets you a job that pays significantly more, then it is worth it. Of course, if you do not earn enough, you will not have to make the repayments and the loan is written off after thirty years regardless of whether you have paid it back and so you could gain a lot even if you do not get a job that pays a lot. However, you need to consider whether you will need other loans on top of that student loan, which have higher interest rates and are therefore more costly. These might be considered to be bad debt.

Bad debt is where you borrow money for items which do not gain you much. Perhaps borrowing to buy clothing or a holiday could be considered to be bad debt.

It is not always easy to tell whether a debt is good or bad. You have to predict the future in some ways to know whether it is worth it or not. You should be able to make some judgements about your future though and how useful the course will be to you.

Think about the type of course you are doing and what career it is leading you too. You may have always wanted a particular job and will need a degree to get it. This could be worth pursuing. However, many people do a degree because they are not sure what job they want and it delays them having to make that decision. It is worth seriously considering whether you fall in to this category. Even if you have started a course, it may be worth you deciding whether it is worth continuing or whether you should consider doing something else or doing a shorter one.

Vocational Courses

If you are doing a course that will lead you directly in to a career then it could be very worthwhile. If you want to be a doctor, teacher, dentist or a vet then you will need a formal qualification. You will need to do the course in order to do the job and therefore it is worthwhile. However, do make sure that you really want to pursue this career and that it seems like something you will still want to do when you have got the qualifications. Most people do not commit to a course like this unless they are sure that they really want to do the job though.

Doing a course like this will mean that you will be far more likely to get a well-paid job. You will get the qualifications needed to set yourself up for a good career and therefore will easily have the means to repay the loan. You will have a great income and so the cost of the loan will be a very worthwhile investment for you.

Other Courses

However, most people will do a more general course, not knowing exactly what they want to do when they leave university. Some courses start off quite general and then specialise towards the end to help to lead you in the direction of a career. It is important that you make the right choices so that you get the qualification and knowledge that you need.

This is where things become more difficult. If you enjoy a subject and feel that you would like a career in it, but are not sure what then taking a degree in it, may not help. It may be possible that you finish the degree and find there are no jobs in this area or decide that you would like to do something else. Some jobs need even more qualifications after the degree has finished. It may be necessary to have an MSc or PhD afterwards or perhaps different qualifications. This can mean a lot more expense and there may not be such good deals on student loans to take advantage of. It can be wise to think carefully about a career path before doing a degree in case you cannot get that job at the end of your course without doing further training.

When degrees were free or at least the course fees were free and a grant could be used by some people to pay expenses, then it was easy to decide to do a course. If you had the prerequisites then you may as well study as it was free. However, these days there is a financial burden to consider when you are deciding whether to do a degree. There may be free education available until you are 18 but after that you will have to pay.

Talk to many people who did degrees at that time and you will find that they will often say that they didn't use it. Obviously a lot of people do use their degree or they got a job that they would not have been able to get without one. This can be dependent on the subject that they studied, the establishment that they attended and whether they were prepared to relocate or do a graduate job when they left. Consider whether you have something in mind when applying for your degree. You may just be encouraged by your school to go on and study more because you are capable of doing so. However, this is not always the wisest choice. It can be better to get in to the workforce and start earning money. You will always be able to go and get qualifications later in life if you think that you need them.

It is worth thinking hard about the debt that you will have and whether you will regret it when you start work or not. Of course, if you get a lower paid job, you will not have to pay back the student loan, but you may have other debts, such as credit cards to pay off. You may also regret spending those years studying when you could have been working and earning money rather than building up debt.

It may be worth delaying doing a course until you have some work experience. You may have a better idea of what you would like to do and then can do a course that leads you there. Many people do courses as they get older and there is no harm in delaying. The saying that you learn better when you are younger is not always true. If you are determined to study something, then you will have an enthusiasm for it. You are more likely to do well. Older people also tend to have better concentration.

It is also worth considering whether it might be better to study part-time rather than full-time. It will take a lot longer to get your qualification, but you could work at the same time. You will be able to earn more money and it might mean that you will not build up so much debt. You may still need a loan for your fees, but you may be able to afford your living expenses without having to borrow any more money.

To Borrow or not to Borrow?

Assuming that you have decided to go ahead with the course, then you need to then consider whether to take out a student loan or not. Some people are in the fortunate situation where they have enough money to pay the expenses without getting a loan. This may be because their parents are happy to help or because they have worked and saved up the money. However, financial advisors would recommend taking out the loan and not paying it back early.

The reason for this is that the loan is a rather good deal. You do not have to make any repayments on it unless you are earning above a certain threshold. Then the amount pay back is determined by how much you earn. So it is a percentage. Then the repayments are taken out of your salary before you are taxed meaning you get a tax break on that amount of money. The loan will also be written off after 30 years, whether you have paid any of it back or just some of it. Some people will have paid it back in full by then, but it will depend on your income. Some people may not have paid any back if they do not get a well enough paid job over the thirty years.

This is very much better than any other loan you can get as you will not have to make repayments if you have no job or decide to stop work to have a family. No other loan would give you this sort of flexibility. It also gets written off after 30 years which again is something that no other loan would ever offer. The repayments will be manageable as they are based on the amount that you are earning. As the repayments are taken out of your PAYE you will also never have to declare it when applying for another loan, such as a mortgage and so it will not have an effect on your credit rating.

There are of course, still some disadvantages of borrowing the money. You will still have the burden of a debt hanging over your head and some people just do not like this feeling. They would rather know that the debt was gone and they no longer have to be concerned with the repayments. It can be better to think of it as a tax rather than a loan and this could help you to worry less about it. The repayments will obviously take away some of your earnings each month and this could leave you short of money. If you go over the threshold of having to make repayments it could mean that your pay rise, actually leads you to having less take home pay. However, this would only happen when you salary just goes over the threshold of when you have to make repayments.

Many people do not realise that you are able to get a maintenance loan as well as a loan to cover the fees. This will vary depending on whether the course is in London and it is partly means tested. There is even a grant available in some cases so make sure that you check to see whether you are eligible as this could really help. Some courses also have full or partial sponsorship, which can also help a lot.

Topping up the Loan

One problem with the student loan is that many students find that it is not enough. The loan should be enough to cover the tuition fees, but some people find that there is not even enough left to pay rent. This is when things can get very difficult and it can be hard to know where to get the extra money from. There is a selection of options and the right one for you, could depend on your own personal circumstances as well as what is available to you.

Borrowing Extra

Borrowing money extra to a student loan should not be taken lightly. There will usually be quite a few offers out there and they can lead to problems in the future. A maintenance loan can be offered to students and this should give extra money but it may still not be enough.

Getting a credit card, for example could lead to a habit of using one a lot and could allow the student to build up a high debt with a high interest rate. It will also be necessary to pay back some money each month by way of a minimum payment. This means that they will be money going out from the start and it could mean that there is not much money left at the end. It can be very easy to just put things on a credit card and not think about having to pay it back. If you get a high credit limit then you could spend a great deal of money and then have to find a way of paying back a big debt when the course is finished.

Using an overdraft can be even more expensive as there are fees as well as the interest to pay. The overdraft will be paid off when money appears in your account. This could be your next loan instalment and you may find that it disappears very quickly if a chunk of it is used to pay off an overdraft. If you use an unauthorised overdraft things can get very expensive and it can be very easy to overspend or not notice that you are getting overdrawn.

Store cards are often available to students. In fact some stores even offer a student discount to entice shoppers. This may look good, but it may also encourage you to buy things that you do not really need. You could end up spending a lot of money in the shop and although you may get a small discount, this could be little help when it comes to finding the money to pay off the store card. You can pay a minimum, like with a credit card, but this will mean you will be charged interest on the card and you could end up having a large expense to have to cope with at some point.

Getting a personal loan could be a cheaper option but often is not something that is offered to students as they have no way of making the monthly repayments until they start work. This is the case with many types of lending.

There are not that many borrowing options out there for students really, because they do not normally have a regular income to make repayments. This means that it can be difficult to find finance. This can be a good thing because it removes temptation and unnecessary expense. However, it can also mean that students have to use one of the expense options available if they do need to borrow money.

If you do decide to borrow money make sure that you check out all of your options. Compare the costs of using different ways of borrowing so that you know which will be the best for you. Consider late payment charges, admin fees and other fees as well as the interest rate when you are considering your options. Think about how you will eventually pay back what you owe and what chance there is that you will be able to do that.

As well as the few think about the lender and whether you think that they will treat you well. Consider whether they might put up the costs of their fees and their interest rates. Think about how good their customer services seem and how good they might be if you have a problem. You may need help if you cannot make a minimum payment and you will need a sympathetic bank to help with this or else you may face even higher costs.

Using savings

Some people may have savings that they can use to help. It can be wise to be careful with these though. It can feel like you have a great buffer so you do not have to be too careful with what you are spending. However, you may need money to fall back on and if you do not get a job straight away you may need it to live off when you finish your course. Therefore make sure that you restrict yourself in how much you spend so that you do not get through those savings. It can be amazing how quickly you can get through a few thousand pounds and not even know where it has gone.

A good thing to do is to calculate that if you wanted your savings to last for the whole of your time at university, how much you would be able to afford to spend each week. So divide the savings amount by the number of weeks of your course and see what you end up with. This could be enough to make you realise how little you actually have, especially if you also want to keep some by for emergencies.

So although having savings can be great, it is wise to be very careful with regards to spending them. Try not to use them if you can manage without and then if you really do need them, they will still be there to fall back on.

Help From Parents

Some students are lucky enough to find that their parents will help them out. This can seem like a great option, but it is wise to be careful. Make sure that you know whether your parents are giving you the money or whether it is a loan. If it is a loan then it may be wise to come up with an agreement as to when it will be repaid and whether interest will need to be paid on it.

Even if it is a gift, be careful not to spend it too quickly or unwisely. There may not be more money where that has come from and so if you come to rely on it then you may find it difficult to manage without it. Some people find it easy to ask their parents for money and some find it hard so consider that when you are spending money that they have given you. You may feel that you can easily ask for more and you may not.

Many children are not that aware of their parents financial situation. If you are relying on them for money, then it is wise to have a better understanding of this if you can. This will enable you to know whether they may be able to give you more money in the future as well as whether you need to consider paying them back, even if what they originally gave you was a gift.

Earning Money

There are pros and cons to getting a job while you are a student. Obviously any earnings will always be useful, as even if the amount of loan you have is enough, it is always good to have some extra money. It is also good to get the work experience. Even if you do not want a job in that particular field when you finish your degree, the fact that you have some sort of work experience, will be in your favour when you are looking for a job. It will show that you are capable of doing a job and this could make the difference between you and another applicant with similar qualifications.

It is important to make sure that the job is well balanced with the work required from university as well. Some courses are full time and so there would be limited time to fit a job in around the work expected outside of classes. Other courses, although full-time have less time expected in the lecture theatre or seminars and so there may be more time available for working. It is best to find out what is expected of the course before planning on working. Perhaps a Saturday job may be okay, leaving evenings and Sunday's to work but any other hours may need to be left for planning until you are sure of the hours expected on the course.

It may be better to do odd jobs, rather than a regular job so that you can do it when you have the time. There are small jobs that you can apply for online. Freelance work, perhaps writing, web design or graphic design may suit you. You may enjoy babysitting or gardening. There are opportunities to do smaller amounts of work which could still help bring in some extra money without you having to commit to doing something regularly that you may just not be confident in doing.

Many students find that a degree course is easier than A-levels and so they do not need to put in as much time and effort as they did then and can fit in a job. However, this very much depends on both the course and the institution and so it is necessary to find out before you start applying or jobs.

In some courses, particularly post-graduate ones, there may be opportunities to earn money within the university. It could be that you can help with research projects being done by other students or professors; you may be able to help with marking or even do some lecturing. This work tends to be quite well paid, although there is often not much of it. It can be easier to fit around your schedule than taking on a job that requires a certain amount of hours a week, each week.

If you do decide to get a job, then it is important that you manage your time well. Make sure that you stay on top of your university work. This is important anyway because then if you find something gets in the way of your university work, perhaps if you are unwell or asked to work extra hours in your job, you will have already done enough to still meet your deadlines. Although most lecturers are flexible with deadlines, especially if you are unwell, you will have to request an extension. It is easier to get the work done early so that this will not be necessary.

How to spend less money

For some people saving money can seem very easy, but to many it is not. We may feel that we spend as little as possible anyway or that we do not want to save too much because we do not want to go without fun. However, there are many ways to save and a lot of them will not prevent you from having fun.

It can be difficult to know where to spend money and where not to, if it is in short supply. Therefore the list of things below is put in order of importance.

Course Fees

Courses do differ in the fees that they charge. There is a difference between the cost of a post graduate course and an under graduate course as well as differences in the costs between different universities.

It is important to consider fees as well as the quality of the course, reputation of the university, location and whether they offer the course that you wish to do. It is wise to approach this in a logical manner. Get a list of the universities that offer the course you want to do and find out how much each costs. Then consider out of those, which you feel offer the best course, are in a location you want to go to and think about the general reputation of the university. Obviously you will also need to have the correct prerequisites for that course, so you may need to eliminate some options if you feel you will not be accepted. Make sure that you visit the universities as well. You will be spending a significant amount of money with them and you want to make sure that your money is being well spent.

Without paying the course fees, you will not be able to do the course. However, if you get a loan for the fees, then it will automatically pay them. You will not have to await for the loan and then use it to pay the fees, they will be sent straight to student services and the fees will be paid. This makes things much easier and saves you from being tempted to spend the money on other things.

If you are using a loan, make sure that you apply for it early though. You do not want to find that you cannot get on a course because you have not secured the finances soon enough.

Rent

Paying rent is one of the most important things that you will need to do. Without rent you will have nowhere to live. You may need to pay the rent in advance or pay it monthly or termly. It is so important to make sure that you have enough money put by for each rent instalment.

When you are choosing somewhere to live, consider the cost. Think about how much your loan is for and how much you will have left once you have paid the course fees. You may have a maintenance loan or other money as well to use towards all of your expenses. It is important to make sure that you always have enough to cover your rent. It may be wise to put all the money that you need for your rent in a savings account that is easy to access so that you will be able to transfer it when necessary and then pay the rent from it. You want to make sure that there is enough.

You may be able to pay the rent in a big block when you receive your loan. This will mean that you will have no worries about having to find the money each month. Whether this is an option will depend on your landlord. However, even private landlords may be happy to accept a lump sum of money to cover a long period rather than hoping that you have the money each month to cover the payments.

It is so important to find somewhere to live that has an affordable rent for you. It can be difficult knowing how much money you will have available to you as well having the time to compare all of the rents. Some accommodation will include bills and food and this could make it easier to manage than ones that do not. However, you may rather live somewhere where you manage these yourself.

Bills

In most accommodation you will be responsible for paying bills. These will be things like electricity, gas, television licence and land line phone. There are ways to save money on all of these.

If you are renting you may not be able to change who supplies your gas and electricity, but it can be worth finding out. Switching to an alternative company may help. You may have a meter for electricity and/or gas and although the rates can be dearer it can make it easier to manage to payments. You will need to buy cards to top up the meter in order to make sure that you do not run out or you will be sent a regular bill to pay.

Happy Frugal Student by Rachel Henderson

If you are sharing accommodation you will need to agree with the others that you are living with how you manage the bills. One person may be happy to pay it if the others give them their share or you may decide to all write a cheque for the amount that you owe. It is worth trying to work out ways to keep these bills down. Make sure that you are using the heating efficiently. Many places have storage heaters and if you do not know how to use them, ask. They do not work in the same way as other heaters and so you could be wasting power using them incorrectly. Check that no one is leaving windows open to let valuable heat out, make sure lights and other appliances are not being left on unnecessarily.

It is not possible to avoid paying for a TV licence just because you are a student. However, check that you need one in the specific place that you are staying. You could avoid the cost by not having one at all. You do need one to watch live television, but to watch TV on Demand you do not and so you could wait to watch TV programmes on your PC, laptop or mobile device and save the cost of the licence. If you are in shared accommodation, you will have to decide whether this is something that you all agree on.

A land line phone may not be necessary these days. It can cost quite a lot to have the line connected and then pay the rental. You will also have to pay for calls of course. Decide whether this is something that is necessary as you may find that it is better just to use your mobile phone, especially if you have a number of calls that you can make within your contract. You may find that parents and friends would rather call a land line because it is cheaper than calling a mobile. It could be worth asking if they will help pay the land line costs so that they can save money in the long run.

Food

Food is something that we all need but there are many ways to make it more affordable. When you are shopping consider the cost of going to that place as well as the cost of the food. If you need to pay for a bus ride or car journey to get to a cheaper supermarket, you may find that it ends up being more expensive over all.

It is worth comparing the cost of supermarkets though. They tend to all claim that they are cheaper, but it will depend on the types of food that you buy. It is wise to make out a typical list of food that you would buy and then see how much it costs in different supermarkets. There is a comparison site that will do this for the main ones but not all are included. It may need a trip to each one to write down the information. It may also mean shopping in different places for different things in order to save the most money.

Certain foods are also a lot cheaper than others. If you look at fruit and vegetables for instance and compare their prices per kg you will soon be able to see which are the cheaper options and which are not. This comparison can be done on all types of food.

It is also useful to note that cooking from scratch is much cheaper than buying pre-prepared food or take aways. This means that having a few cooking lessons before starting university can really help. Just knowing how to prepare a simple pasta dish, baked potatoes, curry, chilli and a few other things would really help to keep costs down. There are some sample recipes in Appendix 1 that might help.

Travel

These days travel can be extremely expensive, whether that means owning a car or using public transport. It is therefore wise to have a think about this before university. Consider what travelling you will be doing. You will probably travel to see family at holiday times if you move away from home. You may need to travel from your student accommodation to the university.

Many universities will run a bus between campuses and from main areas of student accommodation. It is worth finding out whether this is something that you could use. It might even be free to use and could save a lot of money compared to using a car.

If you do decide to get a car then shop around if you are buying one. Try to find a car that is fuel efficient, cheap to tax and insure. A smaller car should fit the bill, but do some research first. Also make sure that the car you buy is in fairly good condition so that you do not have to pay out a lot on repairs if it keeps going wrong.

You should also make sure that you are getting the best deals with regards to insurance. You may find that adding a parent on to the insurance will reduce the cost and also comparing the charges between different insurance companies. You can use a broker to do this for you or a comparison search engine or just do the research yourself getting quotes from different companies.

When you need an MOT or repair, then it could be wise to have it done in the town you come from as you will know more about the garages there than if you choose to go to one close to the university. However, ask around for recommendations as you may find a cheap one and you may need to go to a local one if you cannot drive the vehicle far.

It is also important to find cheap petrol or diesel. There are websites where you can look up local prices and these will enable you to find the cheapest. However, find out the cost of the journey as well as if you travel to far to get fuel then you may be using more money than if you got it at a closer petrol station. Try to drive efficiently too so that you use less fuel. There are many tips online as to how to do this, but by removing unnecessary weight such as roof racks and items in the boot, driving at an average of 50MPH and not accelerating unnecessarily fast, you should be able to use less.

If you are relying on public transport then it is worth looking at student discounts. You may need to purchases a student card for the train or bus if you want a reduction so look at how much you will potentially save and calculate whether it will be worth it. It all depends on how many journeys you make, how much they cost and how much you can potentially save per journey. Using the bus is usually cheaper than the train but it will take a lot longer. You therefore need to consider whether this is a good option for you or not. It will also depend on how convenient the routes are and how often they run a service to the places that you want to go.

Try to reduce the cost of travel by walking as much as possible and cycling. You may also be able to car share with others and split the travel costs that way.

Books & Stationery

Student text books are often very expensive. They can cost a huge amount of money, especially if you have a lot to buy. There are ways to save money on these though.

You should find that there will be copies of the books in the university library. If you cannot afford to buy them, then use them there instead, for free. You usage may be limited as they may need to lend them out to a lot of students.

If you do not mind not having a new copy, but want one for yourself then look out for students selling their books. They may advertise on notice boards around the university. You may also find them for sale online, on auction websites or sites selling second hand books. You may also find them in second hand book shops and charity shops in the town. It can be worth a look around before buying the book new. If you cannot find a second hand copy or really want a new one then shop around. Bookshops can be delightful places but buying books online can often be cheaper. You will be wise to compare the price of the book in the university book shop, high street shops and online to see which will be the cheapest for you. Even if you only save a few pounds per book, this could add up to the equivalent to a free book if you add it up over the whole year.

One you have finished with your books, consider selling them to make some of the money that you have paid back. You may not want to do this with all of your books, but you will find some are more useful than others.

You will also need folders, paper and pens and these can be relatively cheap. However, the cost can add up and so hunt down cheap suppliers. You may find that it works out better to buy in bulk, but make sure that you are confident that you will use all of the items that you have ordered.

Most students have a laptop computer these days. It can be a lot easier, but make sure that you really need it. The university will have computers that you can use and printers. These will be able to be booked and you could use them for free. It can be easier to have your own and you may want them to use for more things than just studying. They can be expensive though so make sure that you look out for any that have student discounts. Search for the right model and brand and then compare prices so that you do not pay more than you have to. It can be worth getting a second hand one as well. Make sure that you only buy a support plan and extra insurance if you feel that it is a good deal for you. You may find that a general student insurance that includes your phone and other belongings might give you a better deal than insuring a computer separately.

Phone

Most people have a mobile phone these days and so it is almost impossible to consider going without. However, the cost of a phone can be really big and so it important to consider whether you really need such an expensive one. Think about what you use your phone for and whether you need all of the functionality that you get.

Firstly consider the telephone calls themselves and whether you really need to make any or whether you can have people call you or use a landline instead. Then consider the text messages and how many you send and how much you pay for them. Also think about the Internet use, if you have a smart phone and whether you need it for this or not. You may be able to use it when you are connected to wi-fi in your accommodation or at the university.

So you need to consider what functionality you need from your phone and then think about what you need to pay for. You may feel you need the calls and texts and therefore want to have a contract to make it cheaper. You may want to be able to surf the web when there is no wi-fi connection and therefore pay for that. This can be expensive though.

Some contracts seem good because they come with a selection of free calls, text and Internet time as well as a phone. However, they can tie you in for a long time and be extremely expensive and so it is well worth considering what you need, what you will use and how much it will all cost. For just a few years it might be wise to get a less good phone with a smaller package so that you can make things more affordable. Once you have completed the course and are earning decent money then you can get a much better one again, should you wish to.

The same goes for a tablet. Decide whether you really need one as well as a phone and laptop. If you already have one then consider not upgrading it until you finish your course so that you can really afford it.

Entertainment

Entertainment is a big part of student life. It is important not to get lonely and to interact with others. However, it can be costly if you go out drinking, for meals and clubbing. It is therefore wise to be careful with your spending.

At the university there will be a lot of clubs and organisations that you can join. These will not be that expensive and so it could be a good way of socialising without having to pay out much money. You will find that there are sports clubs, music, drama and many other things that you can do which will allow you to meet others. These are also a good opportunity to meet people who are studying different subjects to you.

Drinking and partying is as important as study for some. However, try to make sure that it does not cost too much money. Buy cheaper drinks or try to drink them slowly and make them last longer. Restrict yourself to how many times you will go out so that you can help your money to go further or have a budget as to how much you are prepared to spend each month or week.

Insurance

Student insurance is something that some people feel is very important and others do not worry about at all. It can depend on the value of the items you have with you at university and how much of a risk taker you are.

Whether you decide to have insurance is a very personal decision. You may feel that you want to protect your valuables from theft, loss or damage to give you peace of mind. You may feel that the place you are living is risky or that you will just feel better if you have the insurance. When deciding consider what you would do if you had to replace a laptop, tablet, phone, stereo, TV, clothing, books etc. If it was just one it may not be such a burden but if it as all of them it would be. You may be clumsy and want to protect against accidental damage or careless and so need protection against loss.

It is wise to find out the cost of insurance before you decide whether or not to have any. You may find that it is so cheap that you feel it is worth it. Remember to compare different insurers to find out who is the cheapest and what they can offer for the cost. It is not always best to go for the cheapest but it is always wise to compare all of your options to see which provides the best value for money. Consider whether you need all of the services that they can provide for you and this will help you to decide which company to go for.

To compare them you can use comparison websites, brokers or just take a look for yourself.

Other Items

There are other things that you will need as well such as cleaning products, toiletries, clothing etc. There are always odd things that you will need when you move in to new accommodation as well, perhaps a washing up bowl, dish drainer, lamp and things like that. This will all cost money.

If you need personal items, you could ask for them to be given to you as gifts, if you are lucky enough to have friends and relatives that buy you presents on your birthday and at Christmas. You may be able to split the cost of some of the items if you are sharing accommodation. You may be able to avoid buying many new clothes while you are a student.

Student Discounts

Student discounts can seem like a really great thing. It can attract students to shop at particular places but it is wise to be very careful. Most discounts tend to be savings of about 10%. This might sound good, but it means that you might save £3.50 on a £35 pair of jeans. That is still a lot of money to pay. The discount may be very tempting but it may actually tempt you to spend money that you would not have spent because you think that you will be getting a good deal. Be careful in how you approach the discounts.

If you need to buy something, then hunt to find where you can get it cheapest and whether using a place with a discount will help you to save even more. However, there may be places that do not offer a student discount that have the item cheaper than the place that does offer the discount and it is better to buy it without the discount. Make sure that you do the maths and work out how much you will actually be paying for the items.

It is worth bearing in mind which places offer discounts for students and possibly even trying to negotiate a discount even if there isn't one on offer. If you are shopping t places that offer the discount you will know that you need to claim it.

If you go to the NUS Extra website you will see a list of all of the available student discounts with your NUS card. This includes food and restaurants, sports equipment, holidays and travel, department stores, fashion, insurance, music, motoring, hair & beauty and entertainment. There is even an online calculator so that you can work out whether the £12 cost of the card is worth paying compared to the discounts that could be had as a result of it. Most students would gain from it, but it will depend on which places you shop at and whether they offer a discount and so it is worth just taking a look at the places that currently offer a discount to make sure that you will benefit.

Other Discounts

It is possible to get discounts on items that do not offer student discounts but have alternative ones. These will differ depending on whether you are shopping online or offline.

Certain shops have loyalty cards that can allow you to make free purchases in the future. Some supermarkets have these and some stores. It is worth asking in stores that you shop regularly whether they have a loyalty card. Even some Independent shops have it and some local areas have their own local discount card for independent shops. It is worth making sure that you understand how the card works and how you can spend what you are earning while you shop. You may have to accumulate a certain amount or you may be able to take the money off any purchase. It does change from shop to shop. You may also find days when you get better value for the loyalty points that you have earned and so it may be worth waiting to spend them until you have the opportunity to get more money for them.

You will find that shops have sales from time to time. These can also be a great opportunity to pick up some bargains. However, sales can actually be a big problem too. Items that seem so cheap you cannot resist them may be available in the sale. You may find that this means you buy things that you do not need and possibly even not want. It can therefore be sometimes worth avoiding sales so that you are not tempted to buy things that you do not need. However, if there are things that you need, then it is well worth waiting for the sale price to make the most of it.

If you are buying online then there are further opportunities to save money. You can look at cash back sites to see whether you can get a certain amount of the money you spent back again. This could be a lump sum or a percentage depending on the sort of thing you are buying. There are discounts on many things including high street shops, supermarkets, finance such as insurance, holidays and many more. It is always worth a look to see whether you can get some cash back before you make a purchase. You may also find that you can use online voucher codes. These are worth searching for before you make a purchase but may not be able to be used in conjunction with a cash back offer. It is worth checking both though and seeking which will make you the most savings and whether you can combine them together. It is worth comparing different shops and products and take in to account any discount you can get to see where you can get the things that you need for the least amount of money. It is worth doing the research, especially for high priced items, as you could save a significant amount. However, it is so important to be careful when shopping online. They often have offers to tempt you to spend more than you were intending such as free postage if you spend more than a certain amount. This can seem good but you could end up buying an item for £30 just to save £3.95 in postage. It may not be worth it at all.

Savings Account

It may seem rather odd having a savings account as a student. Everyone knows that students do not have very much money to save. However, it can be very useful indeed.

It is so important to have some money put by for emergencies. You may have to travel home suddenly, buy a book, have a car repair or pay some other cost that you did not budget for. By having a lump sum of money tucked away, you will be able to afford to pay for this sort of thing. So when you get your loan or sort out your finances before starting the course, tuck a sum of money away. Try to make it as much as possible. Calculating how much could be difficult but consider how much things will cost and therefore how much you may have to pay out. Think about how much a car repair might be, a train fare home, a selection of books or whatever. Try to plan for any financial emergencies that might happen to you, so that you are prepared.

Having some money tucked away will give you peace of mind. You will know that you have something to fall back on. However, make sure that you do only spend it on emergencies. It is not always easy to leave the money there. Some people like to spend or find it difficult to save and so it can play on the mind and you could keep thinking about it being there waiting to be spent. If you feel that this could be the case with you, then put it in a safer place. Get a joint signatory account so a parent has to sign as well or ask your parents to look after the money for you.

If you manage to have some spare money, then you could top up the savings every so often. This will mean that you will have even more to fall back on if necessary.

Happiness

This can all sound like a lot of hard work and that there will be no fun involved at all. It may look like it adds up to being a frugal student without any of the 'happy' described in the title. However, there are many ways that you can still be happy.

It is important to understand that by being frugal with money and not getting in to unnecessary debt you are setting yourself up well for the future. You will be learning good sending habits and also avoiding unnecessary charges. You should feel very proud of yourself for doing that and let that make you feel happy. Having debts hanging over your head can be miserable.

Happy Frugal Student by Rachel Henderson

Although there are likely to be some debts, the sooner you can get them paid off (apart from the student loan which is a different matter), the better you will feel. So it is important to try to keep those debts down.

Sometimes being frugal will not cause you any differences in everyday life. If you find a cheaper insurance, energy supplier or phone contract you may find no difference at all in your day to day life apart from the fact that you are spending less. It can be worth doing this sort of thing and keeping an eye it every so often. It will only take an hour or so every six months and so is very little effort and leads to having more money.

Other types of saving money may not feel like so much fun. Having to go without new things or not being able to go out as often as you might like, may feel bad. You may not enjoy it at all. However, in the future you will have to miss out on even more if you have large loans to pay back. So even if you do not feel that happy while you are doing all this scrimping, it is important to remember that it will make for a much happier future.

Also getting in to good spending habits right from the beginning can be great for the future. You may decide that you want to buy a house and need to save for the deposit. You may want to save for your retirement. You may want holidays that you need to pay for. You may want a family and have to pay for that. All of these things can be really expensive. If you are already used to being frugal, then you will find saving up for things a lot easier. You are also less likely to have money worries because you spend less. This can help to keep your stress levels significantly lower and will really help you to have a generally happier life.

You can also treat yourself every so often. You could decide that if you spend within your budget for a few weeks then you will go out for a few drinks or something like that. Of course, you could also include a few treats within your budget so that you do not feel deprived.

It is wise to put together a way of spending less that will keep you happy. If cutting out certain things will just be too difficult to bear, then do not do this. However, consider whether you can cut out other things instead. You may decide that you need a few drinks each week, but would be prepared to borrow books from the library instead of buying them to save the money.

It is a matter of finding a balance so that you do not spend too much money but you also have an enjoyable time. Some people get a great sense of satisfaction having saved money. They feel good knowing that they have got good deals. They also have a sense of security knowing that they have savings behind them and the ability to save more money so that they can buy things when they need them and cope in emergencies. They have a happy retirement because they have saved up enough money to pay for it.

Appendix 1

Simple Pasta

Pasta is extremely cheap to buy and you can make a sauce in large quantities that you can freeze or keep in the fridge. This means that you are able to spend some time making a sauce and then keep it in batches to use in the future. You could buy a sauce of course, but this will be more expensive.

To make a simple sauce you will need oil, an onion, passata, dried mixed herbs, salt and pepper. Finely chop the onion and fry in a tablespoon of oil. Use a low temperature and cook it until it is see through. Then add the passata, a teaspoon of herbs and simmer. The longer you cook this, the sweeter the tomatoes will become. However, you could save time and money by adding a teaspoon of sugar. Season with salt and pepper to taste. You can freeze the sauce or keep it in the fridge for a week. You could make a bigger batch by doubling or even tripling the ingredients. Make sure that your pan can hold all of the ingredients though.

Pasta is very easy to cook in a pan of boiling water with some salt added. The packet will let you know how long to coo it for. Once cooked, drain and put back in the pan. Add the amount of sauce you require and heat it through, making sure you stir it so that it does not burn on the bottom.

Bolognaise

There are many ways to cook bolognaise. Find out if you have a family recipe and use that. However, you can use the following recipe instead. You will need 200g mince, 1 tin chopped tomatoes, 1 onion, 1 carrot, oil, 1 stock cube and 2 teaspoons dried herbs. You need to put two tablespoons of oil in the pan and fry the onion, which needs to be chopped finely. Then add the finely chopped carrot. Cook for ten minutes on a low heat and then add the mince and increase the heat. Cook until the meat browns. Then stir in the tomatoes and herbs and crumble in the stock cube. Simmer for 15 minutes with a lid on, stirring occasionally. Serve over spaghetti or with mashed potato. This amount would do for three meals, so two servings could be put in the fridge or even frozen to use later.

Jacket Potatoes

If you have to pay an electricity bill then cooking a jacket potato in an oven can take a lot. Unless you have other things to go in there as well, it is probably better to microwave it. Remove the eyes and stab the skin with a sharp knife. Put in the microwave for five minutes and then stab it. This will be long enough for a small potato. However, if it is larger, you may need another five minutes at least. Stab right through to the centre to feel if it is soft and cook it until it is soft but no longer because it will overcook and go hard and dry.

You can fill the potato with all sorts of things. You could just use butter or cheese but these are expensive. You could use baked beans, tuna, sweet corn or even left over bolognaise. There are lots of options, some more expensive than others and some cheaper than others too.

Vegetable and Bean stew

Vegetables are pretty cheap if you buy them in season. Beans are also cheap, especially if you buy them dried rather than tinned. If you buy them dried you will need to soak them and boil them for a long time to prepare them. It is best to do a big batch if you are doing this and refrigerate or freeze them. Tinned beans are still pretty cheap though.

The stew is easy to make. Peel and finely chop an onion and then add some frozen peas, a peeled and finely chopped carrot and a tin of beans or chick peas. You could also add other veggies that you might need to use up or like such as potato, sweet potato, squash, cabbage etc. You can also add in chunks of meat if you wish to, although these are more expensive.

Easy Curry

Curry can be a really cheap meal and it can also be a good way to use up any food that you have lying around. You can buy a curry paste or curry powder and then it is very simple. Just finely chop an onion and fry it on a low heat in a tablespoon of oil until it is see through, then you can add any vegetables of your choice and meat if you wish. Add the curry powder or paste and then add water, milk or coconut milk to make a sauce. You will need enough to cover half of the vegetable mix. Then you just need to simmer it until everything is soft and cooked through which will take around 20 minutes depending on what you have in it. You can even put it all in a slow cooker if you wish. The spices increase in flavour over time, so if you put some in the fridge or freezer for a later date it will have a more intensive taste. It can be reheated in a saucepan or in the microwave.

Macaroni Cheese

This is a very simple and cheap recipe. The pasta can be

macaroni but the sauce can actually be used on any pasta or even over vegetables, fish or meat. You can make a cheese sauce in several ways. A very easy way, which also happens to be gluten free uses cream and grated cheese in equal proportions just heated up slowly in a saucepan until thick. The more traditional way is to use a knob of butter, melted in a pan and then add a teaspoon of white flour, mix and then add ½ pint milk and simmer for a few minutes before adding grated cheese to taste. The second recipe takes longer and needs you to have flour as well which makes it rather more cumbersome. Both recipes can be prone to lumps, but if you use a whisk to mix them as they cook then the lumps get broken up.

Sausage and Beans

This is such a simple meal it hardly needs instructions. If you buy sausages in a packet, which tends to be the cheaper way to buy them, they will have cooking instructions on. You can even buy microwave sausages if you want things to be really easy. Then you just heat beans in a pan or microwave and serve together.

Appendix 2

To start with you will need to take a note of your fixed income and expenses –

	Money In	Money Out
Loan	£2000 per semester	
Wages	£75 per week	
Rent		£800 per semester
Electricity		£20 per month
TV Licence		£12 per month
Mobile		£20 per month
Insurance		£5 per month

It is not possible to work anything out as the money is not split properly. Therefore start by working out all the costs and income for the whole semester. You will need to multiply the weekly expenses by the weeks in the semester and the monthly ones by the amount of months as below.

	Money In	Money Out
Loan	£2,000.00	
Wages	£1,500.00	
Rent		£800.00
Electricity		£100.00
TV Licence		£60.00
Mobile		£100.00
Insurance		£25.00
Totals	£3,500.00	£1,085.00

Happy Frugal Student by Rachel Henderson

I have added up the totals as well so that you can see that over the five month semester there will be £3,500 coming in and £1,085 going out. This looks really good; having £2415 spare, but you should not start spending madly. You need to calculate how much that is in real terms. It comes out as £483 a month, which is around £120 a week. This money needs to cover all of your variable expenses which include food, travel, entertainment and books. Now it does not look very much at all, especially if you consider how much each textbook is likely to cost. If you have a car to fill up with petrol or are planning on travelling by train home during the holidays, then these are big chunks of money out of that budget. This is why it is so important to work out exactly how much money there is, so that you make sure that you do not start overspending and then find that you have nothing left to pay for food towards the end of the semester.

You may wish to take a chunk out of the £2415 so that you can put it aside to buy books. However, you may decide that you would rather have that money and borrow books from the library.

www.ingramcontent.com/pod-product-compliance
Lightning Source LLC
Chambersburg PA
CBHW071825170526
45167CB00003B/1428